WHY DOES GOD ALLOW SUFFERING?

Why Does God Allow Suffering?

NICKY GUMBEL

KINGSWAY PUBLICATIONS
EASTBOURNE

First published in 1994 as part of *Searching Issues*
This edition 1999
Reprinted 2000

Co-published in South Africa with SCB Publishers
Cornelis Struik House, 80 McKenzie Street
Cape Town 8001, South Africa.
Reg no 04/02203/06

ISBN 0 85476 862 9

Illustrations by Charlie Mackesy

Published by
KINGSWAY PUBLICATIONS
Lottbridge Drove, Eastbourne, BN23 6NT, England.
E-mail: books@kingsway.co.uk

Printed in Great Britain.

Contents

*The issue of suffering is the most frequently
raised objection to the Christian faith.*

Why Does God Allow Suffering?

A young New Yorker named Glenn Chambers had a lifelong dream to work for God in Ecuador. At the airport on the day of departure, he wanted to send a note to his mother but he didn't have time to buy a card. He noticed a piece of paper on the terminal floor and picked it up. It turned out to be an advertisement with "Why?" spread across it. He scribbled his note around the word "Why?". That night his aeroplane exploded into the fourteen thousand foot Colombian peak El Tablazo. When his mother received the note after the news of his death, the question burned up at her from the page . . . "Why?".

The issue of suffering is the most frequently raised objection to the Christian faith. We are constantly confronted by suffering. 'The fact of suffering undoubtedly constitutes the single greatest challenge to the Christian faith, and has been in every generation. Its distribution and degree appear to be entirely random and therefore unfair.'[1]

First, we see suffering on a global scale. There are natural disasters: earthquakes, famines and floods. The suffering that results is often pervasive and arbitrary. The two world wars focused our attention on global suffering in an acute form. As well as these major wars, we are generally aware of at least one smaller war raging somewhere in the world.

Secondly, we see community tragedies. One of the worst disasters in Britain was in Aberfan on 21st October 1966, when a huge coal-tip collapsed and devastated Pantglas primary school, killing 116 children and 28 adults. Almost daily we read or hear of plane crashes, sinking ships or some other disaster affecting the lives of hundreds of people.

Thirdly, suffering at an individual level affects us all to a greater or lesser extent. There is the suffering of bereavement, sickness, handicap, broken relationships, unhappy marriages, involuntary singleness, depression, loneliness, abject poverty, persecution, rejection, unemployment, injustice, fierce temptation and disappointment. Suffering can come in an endless variety of forms and no human being is immune.

It is worth noting that suffering is not a problem for all religions. It is an acute problem for the Judeo-Christian tradition because we believe that God is both good and all-powerful. C. S. Lewis stated the opposing argument succinctly: 'If God were good, He would wish to make His creatures perfectly happy, and if God were almighty, He would be able to do what He wished. But the creatures are not happy. Therefore, God lacks either goodness, or power, or both.'[2]

Theologians and philosophers have wrestled for centuries with the problem of suffering and no one has ever come up with a simple and complete solution. The Bible is primarily a practical book and it never addresses this issue systematically in a philosophical way. What we see are a number of approaches to the problem, all the way through from Genesis to Revelation. There seem to be four main overlapping insights, and we shall look at each of them in turn.

Human freedom

Suffering is not part of God's original created order (Genesis 1-2). There was no suffering in the world before humanity rebelled against God. There will be no suffering when God creates 'a new heaven and a new earth' (Revelation 21). There will be no more crying and no more pain. Suffering only entered the world because Adam and Eve sinned. It is, therefore, an alien intrusion in God's world. If all suffering is a result of sin, directly or indirectly, why did God allow sin to enter the world?

He did so because he loves us and wanted to give us free will. Love is not love if it is forced; it can only be love if there is a real choice. God gave human beings the choice and the freedom to love or not to love. Given this freedom, men and women from the beginning have chosen to break God's laws and the result has been suffering. Again, as C. S. Lewis puts it:

> It would, no doubt, have been possible for God to remove by miracle the results of the first sin ever committed by a human being; but this would not have been much good unless He was prepared to remove the results of the second sin, and of the third, and so on forever. If the miracles ceased, then sooner or later we might have reached our present lamentable situation: if they did not, then a world, thus continually under-propped and corrected by Divine interference, would have been a world in which nothing important ever depended on human choice, and in which choice itself would soon cease from the certainty that one of the apparent alternatives before you would lead to no results and was therefore not really an alternative.[3]

Some of the suffering we endure is the result of *our own sin*. At times, suffering is the inevitable consequence of breaking God's law. There are physical laws of nature; for example, if we put our hand in the fire it gets burned. In this context, pain acts as an early warning system when we exercise wrong choices. There are also moral laws. God made a world built on moral foundations and there is a natural connection between sin and its consequences. If a person abuses drugs, drug addiction may be the consequence. If we drink excessively, we may eventually suffer from alcoholism. If someone drinks and drives a car recklessly and injures himself, his injuries are partially the result of his sin. In a similar way, selfishness, greed, lust, arrogance and bad temper often lead to broken relationships and unhappiness of one sort or another.

Sometimes God actively judges sin in this life. The biblical flood is an example of suffering on a global scale caused by sin, resulting in God's judgement. When 'the Lord saw how great man's wickedness on the earth had become, and that every inclination of the thoughts of his heart was only evil all the time . . . his heart was filled with pain' (Genesis 6: 5-6). In the case of Sodom and Gomorrah, a community disaster was caused by God's judgement of sin. At other times we see God's judgement on an individual's sin (2 Kings 5: 27; Luke 1: 20; John 5: 14; Acts 5: 1-11; 1 Corinthians 11: 30). (For further discussion of the difference between the inevitable consequences of sin and God's active judgement on sin see Chapter 5 under the heading 'Is AIDS the judgement of God on homosexual practice?'.)

It is important to stress that not all suffering is the direct result of our own sin. Job's friends thought Job's suffering must be the result of his sin – but they were wrong (Job 42: 7-8). Jesus expressly repudiates the automatic link between sin and suffering (John 9: 1-3). He also points out that natural disasters are not necessarily a form of punishment from God (Luke 13:

11

1-5). The apostle Peter draws a distinction between suffering as a result of our own sin ('a beating for doing wrong' – 1 Peter 2: 20) and suffering which has no connection with our sin ('unjust suffering' – v 19) or suffering 'for doing good' (v 20).

While it may be appropriate for us to examine our own hearts when we are suffering, we need to be very careful about making judgements about why others are suffering. Church leader David Watson, who died of cancer at the age of fifty, pointed out the dangers of making judgements on others:

The danger about coupling suffering with sin is that the sick person may often feel guilty anyway. Many times I have talked with those who are seriously ill, and I have found them anxiously wondering what they had done to bring about their condition. They blame themselves; or if they cannot live with that, they project their guilt on to others or God. It's someone's fault! The trouble is that either feelings of guilt, which are often imaginary, or direct accusations, which are often unfair, only encourage the sickness. Both hinder healing.

Yet I know how easy this is. Sometimes I have thought of my asthma or cancer as being punishment for sin. I remember with shame many foolish things I have done in the past, and with a fairly sensitive conscience it is not hard to feel both guilty and condemned. The positive side is that every affliction has caused me to search deeply within my heart and to repent of every sinful action or attitude that I could discover. I have known many people who have been dramatically healed following such repentance together with the experience of God's forgiveness. It is no bad thing, therefore, to consider carefully our life in the sight of God in order to know the joy and freedom of his love.

At the same time, the negative side of all this comes when such heart-searching leads to nagging and unhealthy feelings of guilt, and perhaps to a very poor image of God. Is it conceivable, when we see Jesus healing the sick and forgiving the sinful, that God should say, 'Ah, there's David Watson. He slipped up rather badly last month so I'll afflict him with asthma for the next twenty years'? Or later, 'He's upset me again, so this time I'll destroy him with cancer'? Such thoughts are not only ridiculous; they are almost blasphemous, and utterly alien to a God of infinite love and mercy as we see him so clearly in Jesus.[4]

Much of the suffering in the world is the result of *other people's sin*. This is true of many global and community disasters. So much suffering is caused by war, which is always the result of human sin, even if the sin is often on both sides. Much of the starvation in the world is caused by the unequal distribution of the world's resources or by civil war or some other human sin. Even the Aberfan disaster was not a 'natural' one. A five-month enquiry headed by Lord Justice Edmund Davies ruled that the Coal Board was responsible for the disaster. As one woman who contributed to the disaster fund wrote: 'I raged against God, but then I realised it had happened because of man's greed and incompetence.'[5]

Likewise, individual suffering is often caused by the sin of others. So much suffering is caused by murder, adultery, theft, sexual abuse, unloving parents, reckless or drunken driving, slander, unkindness or selfishness of one kind or another. Some have estimated that perhaps as much as 95% of the world's suffering can be accounted for in this way.

This leaves a small proportion which can only be explained as being the result of the fact that we live in a fallen world: a world where all creation has been affected by the sin of human beings. It is the result of Adam and Eve's sin that 'thorns and thistles' entered the world (Genesis 3: 18). Ever since that time 'the creation was subjected to frustration' (Romans 8: 20). 'Natural' disasters are a result of this disorder in creation.

Human freedom does not always answer the question why a particular individual or nation suffers so much, but it does help explain the origin of suffering. All suffering is the result of sin, either directly as a result of my own sin, or the result of someone else's sin, or indirectly, as a result of living in a fallen world.

God works through suffering

Suffering is never good in itself, but God is able to use it for good in a number of different ways.

First, suffering is used by God to draw us to Christ.

God whispers to us in our pleasures, speaks in our conscience, but shouts in our pains; it is His megaphone to rouse a deaf world . . . No doubt pain as God's megaphone is a terrible instrument; it may lead to a final and unrepented rebellion. But it gives the only opportunity the bad man can have for amendment. It removes the veil; it plants the flag of truth within the fortress of a rebel soul.[6]

This has proved true time and again in Christian experience. We meet those who have only begun to think about God as a result of suffering the loss of a loved one, a broken relationship or some other pain in their lives.

Secondly, God uses suffering to bring us to Christian maturity. Even Jesus 'learned obedience from what he suffered' (Hebrews 5: 8). God uses suffering to build our characters. One image used by the New Testament is that of the discipline of children. The writer of Hebrews says that 'our fathers disciplined us for a little while as they thought best; but God disciplines us for our good, that we may share in his holiness' (Hebrews 12: 10). He points out that 'no discipline seems pleasant at the time, but painful. Later on, however, it produces a harvest of righteousness and peace for those who have been trained by it' (Hebrews 12: 11).

Peter uses a completely different image: that of a metal worker refining silver and gold. He writes that his readers may all 'have had to suffer grief in all kinds of trials' (1 Peter 1: 6). He goes on to explain why God allows this: 'These have come so that your faith – of greater worth than gold, which perishes even though refined by fire – may be proved genuine and may result in praise, glory and honour when Jesus Christ is revealed' (1 Peter 1: 7).

God also uses suffering to make our lives more fruitful. Jesus, using a different image on a similar theme, said that as a gardener prunes the vine, so God prunes every fruitful branch 'so that it will be even more fruitful' (John 15: 2).

This again has proved true, time and again, in Christian experience. Smith Wigglesworth, who had a remarkable ministry of healing, said: 'Great faith is the product of great fights. Great testimonies are the outcome of great tests. Great triumphs can only come after great trials.'

David Watson wrote shortly before his death:

There is no doubt that millions of Christians all down the centuries have become more Christ-like through suffering. I know of many who have an almost ethereal beauty about them, refined through pain. In fact those who have experienced more of the love of God than anyone I have ever met have also endured more suffering. When you crush lavender, you find its full fragrance; when you squeeze an orange, you extract its sweet juice. In the same way it is often through pains and hurts that we develop the fragrance and sweetness of Jesus in our lives. An agnostic Professor of Philosophy at Princeton University became a Christian when he studied carefully the lives of some of the great saints of God throughout the history of the Church. What struck him especially was their radiance in the midst of pain. Often they suffered intensely, far more than most other people, yet through all their agony their spirits shone with a glorious lustre that defied extinction. This philosopher became convinced that some power was at work within them, and this discovery eventually brought him to Christ.[7]

A barrister, and now circuit judge, Christopher Compston wrote:

> Over twenty-three years ago, my first son Harry died after only thirty-six hours. At the time, his death seemed monstrously unfair and, in one sense, it undoubtedly was. Now, with hindsight, I am quite certain his death was one of the best things that has ever happened to me in that it began the process of breaking me down so that, with God's grace, I could begin to understand how other people felt and how other people suffered.[8]

Our temptation would be to say to God, 'I'm quite happy as I am. Please leave me alone.' But, as C. S. Lewis points out, that would be to want God to love us less.

> Over a sketch made idly to amuse a child, an artist may not take much trouble: he may be content to let it go even though it is not exactly as he meant it to be. But over the great picture of his life – the work which he loves, though in a different fashion, as intensely as a man loves a woman or a mother a child – he will take endless trouble – and would, doubtless, thereby *give* endless trouble to the picture if it were sentient. One can imagine a sen-

17

tient picture, after being rubbed and scraped and re-commenced for the tenth time, wishing that it were only a thumb-nail sketch whose making was over in a minute. In the same way, it is natural for us to wish that God had designed for us a less glorious and less arduous destiny; but then we are wishing not for more love but for less.[9]

Thirdly, God often uses suffering to bring about his good purposes. Paul tells us that 'in all things God works for the good of those who love him, who have been called according to his purpose' (Romans 8: 28).

We see an example of this in the life of Joseph (Genesis 37-50). He suffered from rejection by his close family, was separated from those he loved and forcibly removed to Egypt, away from his father whom he did not see again for twenty years. In Egypt, he was unjustly imprisoned for a crime that he did not commit. For thirteen years he faced trials, temptations and testing until at the age of thirty he was made ruler over Egypt and was put in a position to save the lives of not only his family, but also of all God's people. Towards the end of his life he was able to speak of his suffering to his brothers, saying, 'You intended to harm me, but God intended it for good to accomplish what is now being done, the saving of many lives' (Genesis 50: 20).

It is not always easy to see at the time what God is doing. Earlier on in his life, Joseph would not have been able to see it so clearly. Often we cannot work out what is going on or why we are suffering in the way we are.

Handley Moule, when he was Bishop of Durham, had the task of visiting the relatives of 170 miners who had been killed in a mining accident. While he was wondering what to say to them, he picked up a little bookmark his mother had given him. As he held it up, on the reverse side of the crocheted bookmark there was a tangled web. There was no rhyme, no reason, no pattern, nothing. But on the other side it said, 'God is love.' The world may seem a tangled web, but behind it all is the love of God.

We have seen that we can begin to make sense of some suffering when we understand that God can use it to bring us to Christ or to help us mature in our faith. Yet this still leaves some suffering which we cannot comprehend or account for in any of these ways.

God more than compensates for our suffering

We see in the story of Joseph how God blessed him in the midst of his suffering. Even as a slave to Potiphar, 'the Lord was with Joseph and he prospered . . . the Lord gave him success in everything he did' (Genesis 39: 2-3). When he was in prison again 'the Lord was with him' (Genesis 39: 21) and granted him favour in the eyes of the chief jailer so that he handed over to him the entire prison administration, 'because the

Lord was with Joseph and gave him success in whatever he did' (Genesis 39: 23). God gave him such remarkable supernatural gifts that even Pharaoh recognised him as a man obviously filled with the Spirit of God (Genesis 41: 38) and put him in charge of the whole land of Egypt (v 41). In this position, he had the joy of seeing his entire family reunited and rescued from starvation.

Job went through catastrophic suffering, losing all his wealth, then all his children and finally suffering from the most horrific disease. At the end of the book we read how the Lord blessed the latter part of Job's life more than the first. As well as great wealth, Job had seven sons and three beautiful daughters. He lived to a great age and saw his children, grandchildren and great grandchildren.

For many, like Joseph and Job, the blessings of God in and through our suffering far outweigh the suffering itself. But the New Testament never leads us to assume that this will always be the case. Rather, every Christian is promised something even greater: the hope of heaven. Paul says, 'I consider that our present sufferings are not worth comparing with the glory that will be revealed in us' (Romans 8: 18), and on another occasion he wrote, 'For our light and momentary troubles are achieving for us an eternal glory that far outweighs them all' (2 Corinthians 4: 17).

Gavin Reid, the Bishop of Maidstone, tells of a boy in his congregation, who shattered his back falling down the stairs at the age of one and had consequently been in and out of hospital. When Gavin interviewed him in church the boy remarked that 'God is fair.'

Gavin stopped him and asked, 'How old are you?'

The boy replied, 'Seventeen.'

'How many years have you spent in hospital?'

The boy answered, 'Thirteen years.'

He was asked, 'Do you think that is fair?'

He replied, 'God's got all of eternity to make it up to me.'

God has indeed all eternity to make it up to us, and the New Testament is full of promises about how wonderful heaven will be. All creation will be restored. Jesus will return to earth to establish a new heaven and a new earth (Revelation 21: 1). There will be no more crying, for there will be no more pain and suffering. We will change our frail, decaying, mortal bodies for a body like that of Jesus' glorious resurrected body. We shall be reunited with all those who have died 'in Christ' and we shall spend eternity together in the presence of the Lord. As Martin Luther once said, 'I would not give one moment of heaven for all the joys and riches of the world, even if it lasted for thousands and thousands of years.'

We live in a materialistic world which has almost entirely lost its eternal perspective. We need to take a long-term view and understand the suffering of this life in the context of eternity. This is not 'pie in the sky when you die'. As the theologian Alister McGrath points out in his book on suffering, that taunt evades the question: 'Is it true?' 'If the Christian hope of heaven is an illusion, based upon lies, then it must be abandoned as misleading and deceitful. But if it is true, it must be embraced and allowed to transfigure our entire understanding of the place of suffering in life.'[10]

God is involved in our suffering

We must be prepared to acknowledge that there is no simple definitive answer to the 'Why?' of suffering. We may approach the problem from a different perspective: God is a God who suffers alongside us.

This fourth insight is perhaps the most important of all. I once heard John Stott say, 'I could never myself believe in God, if it were not for the cross.' God is not a God who is immune from suffering. He is not looking on as an impassive observer, far removed from the suffering world. We see that throughout the Bible and, supremely, we see it in the cross. He is, in Tertullian's phrase, 'the crucified God'. God was 'in Christ', reconciling the world to himself (2 Corinthians 5: 19). He became one of us; he suffered in all the ways in which we suffer. He does not just know about suffering – he has suffered himself. He knows what we are feeling when we suffer.

In 1967, a beautiful athletic teenager named Joni Eareckson had a terrible diving accident at Chesapeake Bay which left her a quadriplegic. Gradually, after the bitterness, anger, rebellion and despair, she came to trust the sovereignty of God. She built a new life of painting (using her mouth to hold the paintbrush) and public speaking. One night, three years after the accident, she realised that Jesus empathised with her completely. It had not occurred to her before that on the cross Jesus was in a similar pain to hers, unable to move, also paralysed.[11]

The playlet, *The Long Silence*, powerfully makes the same point:

At the end of time, billions of people were scattered on a great plain before God's throne.

Most shrank back from the brilliant light before them. But some groups near the front talked heatedly – not with cringing shame, but with belligerence.

'Can God judge us? How can he know about suffering?' snapped a young brunette. She ripped open a sleeve to reveal a tattooed number from a Nazi concentration camp. 'We endured terror . . . beatings . . . torture . . . death!'

In another group a young man lowered his collar. 'What about this?' he demanded, showing an ugly rope burn. 'Lynched . . . for no crime but being black!'

In another crowd, a pregnant schoolgirl with sullen eyes. 'Why should I suffer?' she murmured. 'It wasn't my fault.'

Far out across the plain there were hundreds of such groups. Each had a complaint against God for the evil and suffering he permitted in his world. How lucky God was to live in heaven where all was sweetness and light, where there was no weeping or fear, no hunger or hatred. What did God know of all that man had been forced to endure in this world? For God leads a pretty sheltered life, they said.

So each of these groups sent forth their leader, chosen because he had suffered the most. A Jew, a young black man, a person from Hiroshima, a horribly deformed arthritic, a thalidomide child. In the centre of the plain they consulted with each other. At last they were ready to present their case. It was rather clever.

Before God could be qualified to be their judge, he must endure what they had endured. Their decision was that God should be sentenced to live on earth – as a man!

'Let him be born a Jew. Let the legitimacy of his birth be doubted. Give him a work so difficult that even his family will think him out of his mind when he tries to do it. Let him be betrayed by his closest friends. Let him face false charges, be tried by a prejudiced jury and convicted by a cowardly judge. Let him be tortured.

'At the last, let him see what it means to be terribly alone. Then let him die. Let him die so that there can be no doubt that he died. Let there be a great host of witnesses to verify it.'

As each leader announced his portion of the sentence, loud murmurs of approval went up from the throng of people assembled.

And when the last had finished pronouncing sentence, there was a long silence. No-one uttered another word. No-one moved. For suddenly all knew that God had already served his sentence.[12]

The knowledge of his suffering removes what Jürgen Moltmann has called the 'suffering in suffering'. We are not alone in our pain. When we suffer, he suffers with us.

How do we respond to suffering?

When we are suffering we will not always be able to work out why. God never told Job why he was suffering, but he told him there was a good reason. He pointed out that Job knew very little about the universe and asked him to trust God. The book of Job is not so much about why God allows suffering as it is about how we should respond to suffering.

The questions we need to ask ourselves are these:

First, 'Is this suffering a result of my own sin?' If it is, we can ask God to reveal the specific sin. God will never leave us with a nebulous feeling of guilt. That kind of condemnation may come from Satan, but never from God. If there is a particular sin, we need to repent and ask God's forgiveness and cleansing.

Secondly, we need to ask, 'What are you saying to me through this?' There may be some particular lesson God wants to teach us.

Thirdly, we need to ask, 'What do you want me to do?'

Next, we need to hold on to our hope. This life is always a mixture of battle and blessing, and in times of battle, we need to remember that they do not last for ever and often blessing is just around the corner. Whether it is or not, we can be sure that one day we will go to be with the Lord for ever. Meanwhile, we need to keep our eyes fixed on him (Hebrews 12: 2), knowing that he is more than able to sympathise with us as he has suffered more than we ever will.

When we see others suffering, we are called to show compassion. In the face of great suffering, attempts to rationalise can be counter-productive. Even if their suffering is caused by their own sin, we are in no position to throw stones. We are all sinners, and we need to be very careful about making judgements. Not all suffering, as we have seen, is directly related to sin. Usually, the most positive thing that we can do is to put an arm around the person and 'weep with those who weep' (Romans 12: 15, RSV).

We are right to resist suffering because, as we have seen, it is an alien intrusion into God's world. Jesus fought against suffering wherever he came across it. He fed the hungry, healed the sick and raised the dead. He saw his ministry in terms of preaching good news to the poor, proclaiming freedom to the captives and recovery of sight to the blind and releasing the oppressed. We are called to follow in his steps.

Finally, and in summary, we need to come back yet again to the cross of Christ. For it is here that we begin to understand why a God of love should allow suffering.

First, we see that human beings abused their God-given freedom when they chose to nail Jesus to the cross. And yet God used that very abuse, enabling Jesus on the cross to pay the price for that sin, and for all sin through all time.

Secondly, we see God working through suffering. Those who nailed Jesus to the cross intended it for evil, but God intended it for good. The cross is ultimately a victory because it holds the key to salvation.

Thirdly, we see that God more than compensates for suffering. Jesus 'who for the joy set before him endured the cross' (Hebrews 12: 2) saw ahead to his resurrection, and as a result of that, to our own resurrection and eternity with him.

Fourthly, and most important of all, we see that God himself is not removed from suffering. He participated in the suffering of the cross and he suffers for us and with us now.

FOR FURTHER READING

C. S. Lewis, *The Problem of Pain* (Fount).
John Stott, *The Cross of Christ* (IVP), especially chapter 13.
David Watson, *Fear No Evil* (Hodder & Stoughton, 1984).

NOTES

1. John Stott, *The Cross of Christ* (IVP, 1986), p311.
2. C. S. Lewis, *The Problem of Pain* (Fount, 1940), p14.
3. *Ibid*, p59.
4. David Watson, *Fear No Evil* (Hodder & Stoughton, 1984), pp114-115.
5. *The Times* (19th October 1991).
6. C. S. Lewis, *op cit*, pp81, 83.
7. David Watson, *op cit*, pp119-120.
8. Christopher Compston, *Recovering from Divorce*

(Hodder & Stoughton, 1993), p142.

9. C. S. Lewis, *op cit*, pp30-31.
10. Alister McGrath, *Suffering* (Hodder & Stoughton, 1992), pp100-101.
11. Joni Eareckson and Joe Musser, *Joni* (Pickering & Inglis, 1976), p96.
12. John Stott, *The Cross of Christ* (IVP, 1986), pp336-337.

Alpha

This booklet is an Alpha resource. The Alpha course is a practical introduction to the Christian faith initiated by Holy Trinity Brompton in London, and now being run by thousands of churches throughout the UK as well as overseas.

For more information on Alpha, and details of tapes, videos and training manuals, contact the Alpha office, Holy Trinity Brompton on 020-7581 8255, (home page: http://www.alpha.org.uk), or STL, PO Box 300, Kingstown Broadway, Carlisle, Cumbria CA3 0QS.

All the books are available from your local Christian bookshop, or in case of difficulty contact Kingsway Publications, Lottbridge Drove, Eastbourne, E. Sussex BN23 6NT (01323 437700).

Alpha Hotline for telephone orders:
0345 581278 (all calls at local rate)

Kingsway Publications

Alpha

Alpha titles available

Why Jesus?   A booklet – given to all participants at the start of the Alpha course. 'The clearest, best illustrated and most challenging short presentation of Jesus that I know.' – Michael Green

Questions of Life   The Alpha course in book form. In fifteen compelling chapters Nicky Gumbel points the way to an authentic Christianity which is exciting and relevant to today's world.

Searching Issues   The seven issues most often raised by participants on the Alpha course: suffering, other religions, sex before marriage, the New Age, homosexuality, science and Christianity, and the Trinity.

A Life Worth Living   What happens after Alpha? Based on the book of Philippians, this is an invaluable next step for those who have just completed the Alpha course, and for anyone eager to put their faith on a firm biblical footing.

Telling Others: The Alpha Initiative   The theological principles and the practical details of how courses are run. Each alternate chapter consists of a testimony of someone whose life has been changed by God through an Alpha course.

Challenging Lifestyle   Studies in the Sermon on the Mount showing how Jesus' teaching flies in the face of modern lifestyle and presents us with a radical alternative.

30 Days   Nicky Gumbel selects thirty passages from the Old and New Testament which can be read over thirty days. It is designed for those on an Alpha course and others who are interested in beginning to explore the Bible.

All titles are by Nicky Gumbel, who is on the staff of
Holy Trinity Brompton

——— ❖ ———